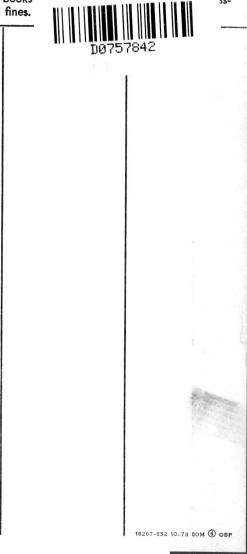

ANOTHER
KIND
OF
RAIN

ANOTHER KIND OF RAIN

Poems by
GERALD W. BARRAX

University of Pittsburgh Press

ISBN 0-8229-3206-7 (cloth)
ISBN 0-8229-5218-1 (paper)
Library of Congress Catalog Card Number 75-117470

Henry M. Snyder & Co., Inc., London

Manufactured in the United States of America

Some of the poems in this book have appeared in *Colloquy, Journal of Black Poetry, Out of the War Shadow* (1968 Peace Calendar), and *Prologue*.

"Nude as Cassandra," "Nude with Apple," "Nude with Tumblers," all from "Five-Part Invention," and "Two Poems" originally appeared in *Poetry*.

"Second Dance Poem," "I Called Them Trees," and "Your Eyes Have Their Silence" first appeared in *The Young American Poets* edited by Paul Carroll, copyright © 1968 by Follett Publishing Company.

The epigraph on page 46 is from *The Myth of Sisyphus and Other Essays* by Albert Camus, translated by Justin O'Brien, © 1955 by Alfred A. Knopf, Inc. Used by permission.

The epigraph on page 65 is from *The Rule and Exercises of Holy Dying* by Jeremy Taylor, edited by Thomas Kepler. Used by permission of World Publishing Company.

The line "Hotter than a pepper sprout" on page 8, from "Jackson" by Billy Edd Wheeler and Gaby Rogers, is used by permission of Bexhill Music Corp.

The four lines on page 77, from "Things Ain't What They Used to Be" by Ted Persons and Mercer Ellington, are used by permission of Tempo Music, Inc.

For All My Live Ones

Publication of this book has been aided by a grant

from the A. W. Mellon Educational and Charitable Trust.

Contents

FORECAST

.

Efficiency Apartment

My sons.
sometimes I can / not name you
until this magic room is sleeping
and the stretched out ends our lives make
curl around
and stitch you thru the interstices
behind my eyes.

*

> (And ceremonies changed us
> And equaled what we became
> And ceremonial words preceded us
> Into flesh and spirit and aborted us
> Into the ends our lives made
> With marvelous cadences to tell us what we were
> And would be.)

*

One, Two, and Three
when the room is awake and shrugs the shadows off its walls
I see the papered magic I've added
    scraps left over from the ends the world made.
Roger is jolly on the wall and says hi
Hippity Hop skips under the breast of a dragon's shadow
    that burns yellow leaves in green flame

    the moonmen's marbled earth
    (that I gave your names to remember me)
floats in space above the telephone

and what you drew and gave me once on a visit
  One, your seraped boy with the cactus grin
  Two, your Sopwith Camel firing four lines
    of wavery pencil rounds into the dragon's mouth
      (I arranged it that way to conserve the forest)
  and Three's cycloptic snaggletoothed house

I call children's art when visitors ask

            *

    (Dear, lost, penultimate love
    Poorer for, richer for rituals
    Of birth and mortgage
    We made formality of ceremony
    And two or three and ten years
    Was too long to live the deaths
    That did us part.)

           *

Your schoolday weather.

    (Did she know the probability of rain?)

Winter mornings close the room.
She wakes you before leaving
  and unthreads you from my sleep.

    (Did she hear the forecast at all?)

Twelve and ½ miles and one river
is close enough to dress you in three warm apologies

        for being here.

In bells and voices at noon
in the center of a cross
                    of church, funeral home and two schools
it opens   and   I am imprisoned
by the shouting sons of other fathers

playing (

                    *

Did I play with you?

          (We gave us One for our youth
          Two for love
          Three the image of me.)

Is a father with no sons
a nursery with no rimes
songs, music
now
roses no rings
but ashes   ashes
down the hill we fell
rolling One   sliding Two   tumbling Three

out of the ends of our lives

now

I am black sheep
three boys empty

I will go hi
        (Spy in her eye)
round my base is

round my base
   hidingO seekand
daddy's
(*find me!*)
(lost)
  it

           *

     (I wed thee
     I ring this with what we were
     In seeming real
     One   in
     Two   seemly
     Three black
           sons.)

           *

Books all over the place

my little people   big people
slim and fat   —boys

daddy does well in school—

they hunch in bookcase caves
and a box under the table
and squat on top of the closet
in my efficient kitchen

they are a comfort these days
chatting away in my unsleeping
exorcising the square deific

After opening the doors out of your lives
  boys
      I followed the little people leading the piper

and here I am
12½ miles and one river

  wondering:what if I kill them

will they drown or burn

                              and then?

But no I guess
I have already given my only begotten sons
to save them
            and
every week
it seems
I buy at least one
more

                  *

Hello.   Hello.   Hello.

and to make him laugh I play my old game

      Is that you, Sam?

I have no son by that name.

It was funnier when
they'd come home from
school and I'd keep
them waiting outside the
back door asking who
they were *Is that
you Sam Harry Joe?*
and they'd fall all
over each other shrieking

no daddy
it's *us!*

Hello,Hello.   hello.
what were you doing
how is school
are there grapes on the vine yet
I'll see you soon   I dont know
goodnite goodnite goodnite
no   tell her goodnite for me

*

(Even now
The cadence of our changes remains in phase.
I had only to become what I am
And you what you will not.
Hotter than a pepper sprout.
I am learning to play the guitar you gave me
Trying not to smoke
So much.
Peace. Your hold forever
And now speak.)

*

Here we go round
here we go round
the Supremes hover above my feet
    the 3 girls I'll never have
the telephone is sorry
the room is raining, efficiently
the room rains and rings
the ends are stitched together
One, Two and Three
                    will be fine
the fit will survive

I have made us all typical
now
true to myself
the nigger daddy for social statistics

(is it asleep?   yes
sleeping and raining and ringing)

goodnite   goodnite   goodnite
Dennis   Jerry   Josh

II DROUGHT

Drought

This could be the way
the fire comes: God's
fine irony withholding rain.
We could wait for the comfort
of overstatement
(half the Flood was tears)
such as something going out of orbit,
as something falling into the sun
as another kind of rain,
but where is His hand in fire
if the woods are dry?

The woods are dry.
Leaves curl, brown,
fall from God's head
and crackle underfoot like irony's laughter.
At twilight a forest burns
and the sun goes down in more splendor
than even God gave it.
Only I am its match.
My roots need rain, too,
but neither rain nor fire
tells me if it is man or god who is chained to this rock.

Poem

That black bitch of a muse I had refused
To touch me with her fire when I had to sing
In the dead silence of sterile white space
And she's gone, selling it now, because I couldn't pay her price.
But I missed her even after she called me
A jive nigga talkin' and writin' trash
I missed her until I knew what I knew before
When I had straddled her in such uncertainty—
That a poem is the loneliest thing in the world,
And the cruelest,
The means for tearing the soul from humanity.
And now with out her

I find myself wrapped in self
Embrace
And wild to hear my soul's applause.

[Untitled]

Goddamn if we move and water crystallizes
or even think it   speak it
and spring dies with its birds
then goddamn we ought to know not
to think to speak to make us move

knowing that but we are moved anyway
it is in whispers as children
kids, rather
secrets from somebody bigger
goddamn
who hears and fucksusup

and the underbelly of heaven freezes
                                        over seas
and the goddamn troop ship skates
                                        across the Pacific
and in the evening
the geckoes sing in the trees like birds

and in the morning
the birds sing in Tagalog

and in the without   you
I short-time in town
and laugh
and grow strong

   and understand nothing

First Dance Poem

In our time there were musicspheres that made the sound
    for us to dance, to touch.
      We could hear to touch.
What we imitate should grow (because) flesh is mother of grass
    (but) our dances imitated planets
      instead. Now they dance the new way
the only way not to touch. They have discovered the use
    of empty space   committed to empty space (&)
      space of bodies   they sculpture the air
between them with suggestions of innocence.
    There is no other way for them
      not to touch.
The gods speak thru their oracles
    fingerpoppin' screaming soul bluehued sound
      interpreted by their high priest
"This is the number five sound this week
    baby."
      The virgins of their temples
dancing the new way with one partner
    or another or none
      make us remember
dry grinding under hot blue lights
    and their suggestive innocence is disconcerting.
      they dont touch.
But the fairways are lush and green anyway and fields as luxuriant
    as the way the hair grows free and shows
      the grass how to grow. The flesh that mothers grass.
Then they who have forsaken the old ways of touching

    dance

their way the Dances
of the Cattleprods   of the Burnedcars
    of the Snarlingdogs   of the Firehoses
        of the Nightsticks   of the Lockups
and then they touch. They have the touch to see
    and our innocence makes them cover their eyes.
    They show us we could just as well dance
the new way and show the grass. The touch
    the flesh that mothers
        it

Second Dance Poem

This (vestige of woman's animalness is the open secret that
  riddles & ruins me &
    cheated of the evidence by
shaved limbs & armpits I bless the perversity of those
    whose arms & legs trap
  beads of light & break
them into component hairs. Ruined by riddles too I see
  the gesture of her walking
    & dancing & think of
the way her brush does invisible things to the air .
  Draws . Paints . with the artistry
  of the part-woman civilized
by cosmetic sterility. A little madly because it ruins me
  I think away what she
    wears hoping to think that
her wiry   silky   tangled   feathery   or whatever she denies climbs
  her belly & spreads over
  her thighs like wheat fire
night or earth. & even hangs bearded from the triangle
  that begins & ends my
    doom. Because I'm no good
at riddles.
      The gesture of her knees is another kind
    of dance . . . a Sacrifice. I
  go because her glory doesn't
crown but conceals & she hides so beautifully I'm reluctant
  to find her. I think
    of being lost & having
to part through the cushion that breaks the fall &
    sudden stop of flesh , going
  into not what is hidden
but what hides. What she wears or denies is not
  enough.

There is this fear
each time: that the resident
beast of her jungle will not be the friendly mongoose
I expect, but an avenging
vicious half-lion & I will be skinned
& sacrificed because I'm a
failure as a tempter & no good at riddles.
Call it what you will
but it)
ruins
me.

To a Woman Who Wants Darkness and Time

where light is
where your body is blacker
where light is

where love lights love
out of sight
of all other reason

we will take the guts out of night
and lay its old breezes and moons
on the altars of afternoons

where light is
where your body is blacker
in a room in the sun

if this is treason
compound it in a room with wrens and sparrows
streaming dust in stiletto beams

like flecks of sun
we will be striped and bound
and listen to nightingales dying

But first we must sit in intellectual talk
and smile across a room
and walk around the edges of your years

And I will tell you about time
lover please
listen

New grass springs from reluctant
as well as eager lovers
ultimately a mass

of melting flesh brings
spring   yes   spring
and hell

while waiting to glisten in dewdrops
on grass from melting
flesh

woman   lover   mine
melts   now   now
hush   ah hush   then

when it stops
may my prodding of you
answer me with spring
If you would live in my untrodden ways
where the judgment of the body
is valid as the mind's

and lovers are garroted by twisting eyebeams
and the moon strangles in its own congealed blood
and an hour forgets nothing years remember

but tell me that love must wear yellow leaves
and I will build pyramids for you of robins' eggs
and mountains of aspen leaves

It will come
when we are covered with the yellow leaves of God's head
shedding

it will
and I will remember the carnage
where light is the black taste of your body
between my savage teeth

Filibuster, 1964

for a number of Senators

Knowing all the ways Black men die
we hold back the impulse to laugh
when jackasses debate our existence.

If Samson slaughtered a thousand men
with half your equipment
and our benevolent Sam has eighteen of you
and one rebel pachyderm in his southern stables
who intend to surpass Samson's kill a thousand times
simply by talking us to death

we don't laugh.

If you're offended by "jackasses"
remember it's your party
and the shibboleth and masquerade you've made of it
have forked your tongues
and betrayed the fraud of braying our deaths
for tradition's sake
in the voices
of the image
you call God.

What could we expect.
We lost the luxury of disbelief
too long ago for surprise
too soon to suppress the prophetic horror
that you will talk now   now even knowing
the bastard you get from delay may be Death.

Spring will overtake you in the Senate
while we move toward the splendor
   and fury
      of the kind of summer
         your surprise admitted
only last year.

(When for your amusement
we seduced your bullets into our backs
and consecrated the churches your god built
to your bombs)

While you talk
we discover better ways of dying
than you ever invented for murdering boys.

      Boys! Boy / that really kills you
      like pulling the trigger
      thinking the thing is pointed at me
      and finding yourself with more shattered images
      that bring luck and me another 100 yrs.
      Boy / equal to the noble use
      you've made of a war and civil filibuster

Talk another summer to death
and we may quibble among the ruins of your rhetoric
after the plague on both your houses leads
both black and white
down the path of your prattling glory.

When you have done
and your last shard of eloquence falls
                              from
                              the
                              air
the applause you'll hear will be the one hand clapping
of your hooded constituent
horribly grinning in the gallery.

The Scuba Diver Recovers the Body of a Drowned Child

Maria, she said. No city river
Should take a name like that.
You should have been an island child and dived or fallen
Into water that liquified sunlight. Once,
    in the Bahamas, Maria, I saw
a school of fish frightened by the shadow of a plane.

There aren't enough Marias
Even in the Caribbean with all its light
To give one of you to this waste and muck.
Did you die in the taste of mills and factories? And
    when the shadow passed
over the clear water I was swimming among them.

How much of your life was there to see
To make you almost forget to breathe?
It was here, waiting for you. Scenes
Passing out of all our lives into yours. Bright
    sun. The painted fish
swimming in and out of the coral around me.

Your mother said . God . here under the river .
You were a beautiful girl she said.
All our lives have passed. Your black world blacker
Here where the sun never reaches. Next
    summer the sands will be whiter   I will go down deeper
without my mask   and come up and let the air suck my lungs out

when we go up   Maria
she will arrange your hair
and the wind will dry it
sun warms you
she said you were beautiful
she will know

Five-Part Invention

Keep up your bright swords, for the dew will rust them.

Shakespeare, *Othello*

I NUDE AS CASSANDRA

I had no need to be Juliet's deatheyed boy
in this age of tragedy for the common man
but the news media chronicle it and make chaff of
living as if death were not more common than man
with the homage of pity and terror that belongs to life.

And love. And death ends life   tragedy   and love
in anticlimax to all the pity
and terror it takes to love and breathe. We wanted
deserved bright swords in this little time of
reducing to anonymous traffic statistics by the National

Safety Council the catharsis of the age. Bright swords
for which we had no more to give than all
we belonged to had to lose in us   a risk
that once would have won us the destruction of an ancient
innocent Troy   now in domestic law

tried for desertion, assessed for child support.
We had no names to give us immunity from the colors
of our eyes and only where we were made the
mornings heavy enough with dew to extinguish
crosses. Somewhere among the hills she strummed

her guitar and sang to me of wind and rain.
I stopped listening, followed and brought her back hoping
for something tragic for those who let us go
and stopped her singing with kisses praise and promises
with one eye on the swords that hung above our heads.

II NUDE WITH APPLE

She would expect any fool to
flatter her but she didn't know
she had places untravelled by praise
where simile nor metaphor were
praise enough to reach. Her sighs
(she knew no better than any wide
eyed girl than that) should have been weary
with words and mine were no more than
any mother's son loving mother
still had seen and not seen, too near
to see or touch in her raging body:
her perfect skin   incredible thighs
(where meeting in all her brownsilked sweetness
there was more need for love than praise)
and breasts too small for anything but
an abstract like beauty whose warm
faces budded with praise in far
less surprise than hers: the curve of
genesis her hips made was the end
the perfection of all creation, all
finished and closed within their sphere
where all to be was curved and rounded
as her hips, sweeter again than Adam's
naming or my praising could tell.
And oh her eyes. Her eyes. Her. Eyes.

III NUDE WITH FLOWERS

I promised her probable things
I knew were mine to give with less
Certainty than sorrow and love
For her doublecrossed heart—the heart

That made promises so casually
Made flower and grow terrifically
Lavish, even wearing them as
Flowers, visible, her new

Extravagance becoming her
So well she thought to say to those
Who saw her disarray and cloud
Of hair as she ran to where I

Was, "I don't care. I'm his girl."
She walked into our rented room
To see and be the things I'd said.
"Teach me," she said, "not to hurry.

"Teach me not to reach and hurry
And try to catch my ringaround
Merrygo. Slow me. Oh slow me."
So she came and wrapped me in her

Hasty hair and rubbed me with it
Everywhere to warm my blood and
See if we could teach the terror
Of love to those whose love we praised

For being there. She flowered there,
Remembering promises, made
The room tremble with her waiting—
And oh her eyes. Her eyes. Her. Eyes.

IV   NUDE WITH SEAWEED
Outside the high room
where the Ohio sprang from two rivers
at the Golden Triangle
   I gave her   made her
     oceans & seas
    big enough to drown us
wherever there was white sand
beaches , birds to clap her hands

lovely as she was
the rivers took us from the city's waste
to high air   salt   bright & clean
to break the heart.

I have willingly drowned a little
in bodies of water & women
(once   (when I was younger & believed in words
       they said it wouldn't be over my head
       and I jumped. It wasn't true:
       the blur of all my tall days
       until Eddie's hand like God's
       reached thru the blue sky & water
       wedded for my dying.

And I know that if she were the sea
she would be choked with suicides
if she wed herself to the sky
for each drowning in her earth
embracing body

And I know that the blood
sounds the same in near death and love
in that mindless space
                    the impact on the organs
before it flows back
but what makes it go there
at all
      God
what makes it not
                    go?
                         Hero: *My love, will you not drown*
                              For love of me?

                         Leander: *O my lady I try O*
                                   I try!

            Her
body submerged.
Undulating
arched.
And surely gaping
the first time
openmouthed I
should have swallowed & gushed
the ocean itself. I love
you O
I said & she
waited & arched & undulated
       in the high room
          we opened the blinds to the turning birds
          and I waded at the edge of the sea
between the white sand & sun.
    Thrashing   her   soft   thighs
    she undulated   arched   swam

out there waiting for me
and I waded little by little unable to swim into the sea
hearing her think of promises.

But I love
you (she   only waited
hush
        now. Later.

We lay covered from the dry floor
her softness scissoring me
(soft . think . only flesh)
bedsoft now remembering promises.
Reading erotica I suggested to her
for the sake of

me.   (What is the sound of time in the blood?
          Keep reading. Keep
          reading. There.   Now

                    Isolde: *We sail to my husband.*
                            Better we return
                            To Ireland or cast our-
                            selves into the sea.

                    Tristan: *There is no drowning for*
                             me.
                             I will die in sight
                             of you and the sea.

                    She
called from the middle
of the water. The sun
sank lower and still
between her and drowning
and me. This time I pulled her out.
With me. I
saved her.

When the sun was gone
there was no sun but her.
We brought the moon from the wall.
We talked face to face
We held
hoping for catastrophe
flood, tidal wave
on the pillow.
We laughed discovering each other as children
growing up. I was a beamish boy.
We grew in minutes to the room.
I love
thee. The silence we stared into.
And my silence poised at the edge of her waiting
   breaking over the crest and falling
      down and closing itself in her . eyes

               Helen: *My husband will follow us*
                       to Troy
                  Across the wine-dark sea.
                  There will be death and
                       destruction
                  Because of you and me.

               Paris: *The sea is calm.*

The third time under near death and love
the blood sounds / down again
and I sank for her center of gravity
  where I would never be seen
    on the face of the earth in
      any eyes but hers   seeing
       the rest of our lives beyond the room
this time
        the sea in her wedded to our electric moon

I was there
and touched the bottom of the deepest promise (O
slow me)   the nearest deep to swim or crawl from
          back to land   & yes
Yes she said you
are O and O
fuck me & I couldn't stay but
shot up, buoyant
fighting the pull of the rocking earth
    and busybody tidal moon in the socket by the bed
screaming
knowing I would see in her
my life no more
no more
no
coming up through the salt
(I love thee
washed up   out   of her
eyes

                    Outside the high window
                    gulls flashed white wings
                    in the moonlight turning
                    as her hand turned and curved
                    down into the harbor
                    where the empty boats rocked
                    with the pull of the moon
                    waiting for morning to put to sea
                    trailing nets
                              & swooping birds

V NUDE WITH TUMBLERS

I had wanted to see you sleeping. We had
Hours and world enough in that little time.
In that high place hours enough to feed and tame
What raged in us. Hours enough to place your head
Within my arm where I could breathe and mouth
Your hasty hair and the sweet proof that the myth
Of your sisters and my brothers, as sad

As what it meant to us, was true. Your small
Hand making the random secure movements of a child,
Sleeping, on my chest. You warm against the cold
Expense of the room. Against me. I would smell
The warmth of your sleep. Now. Here. After. And what
Ever ritual your waking I would wait
O my life for your sleep and my death to recall.

The hours but not the time for sleep. We lay
In wait like desperate vampires for the smell
Of my blood under the sheets turgid in the feel
Of your hand. For my own hands I could not destroy
The picture that now provides my private hell.
Nude in motion smiling seeing me kneel
As you come from the bathroom with the glasses. I pay
With my hands your picture and price for fidelity and stay
Just ahead of my need. For thinking I will
Forget goddamn you after all for the fool
I expect to be like any moisteyed boy
Mourning his first love. Those swords in the chill
Morning of our love tarnished by dew as cool
As your eyes undeserved and put away. They
Decay, diminishing in brightness each gray day.

Two Poems

GUNSMOKE: 1957
    Sun
day afternoon in the Philippines on
Clark AFB in '57 I remember how the
    sun
was like a pane of glass cleaned to invisibility
and walking somewhere between guarded fences in that
    sun
with my radio who but William Conrad
the deep orchestral voice we knew as
the first Matt Dillon disclaiming on
Columbia Radio Workshop brought to me
in that
    sun
by the AFRS that maxim about a picture and 1000
words by reading as a solo instrument from a
Japanese poet who will remain anonymous
to me
what silence is:

The butterfly sleeps on the temple bell.

That was the challenge that only Conrad-Dillon
could have made before the giant his voice created,
the duel in the
    sun.
between us.
He was magnificent. He smiled his sad chancy

smile at my stopping on that glass road just
to stand still and turned his back to me and
rode into the rising sun.
It never occurred to him or me when I could have
charged it against him how absurd their sleep is:—
how it murders sleep and silence for man in or out
of the
   sun more insidiously than Macbeth's bloody dark.

BUTTERFLIES: 1965
Now, Matt Dillon,
love has come for
me, gone for her
and they color the
eyes to the wind
blue yellow white
in the fruited air
in their silence
and soft furor with
wings demurely drawing
down and up contours of
air and
    sun,
contradicting the kind of beauty of raucous birds.
How we have changed! Seen now, you less authentic
to the eye than ear, they in silence as a medium
that made their rare ugliness as worms at least in-
visible to the ear and I in the wrong season revers-
ing their metamorphosis. Where once I drew the wind
and
    sun
for her, gaudy and
raucous, frantic for
summer as a mayfly, I
now make love for her
more beautiful in this
cocoon of silence.

A Pause of Silence

Sometimes the city lets me
                    dream
a green blaze of wildness
as a green lover
as the green lover
              I am
embraced by her need   to be seen
embraced by my need   to be stunned
                              as a virgin
in a green lover's limbs.

Sometimes the sea's mad thing
                    I cry
over it in the voices of gulls and herons
frenzied for sea
              sound
and the after taste of salt.

It rains
wet neon autumn
colors ripple
in the streets
I am maddened only by the small buzz of flies
and nature walks for me
on
one
leg
and the pigeons, the pigeons
take my heart away from hawks.

I Called Them Trees

The last time
            I went to the library
I looked at the flowers
surrounding the statue of Steven Collins

Foster and the old darkie ringing
        the banjo at his feet
                        :flowers planted
in four triangular beds
alternating red and white.
But I saw they were all the same kind.

There were others
                in front of the building
in long wide rectangular rows
bordered by round clusters of pastel green
and white that were too deep, too dark
        red, maroon, for easy images
                        :I called
them all flowers.
And the stunted trees I
wished I had known, bending over the green

terrace above the flowers
    like women whose faces
I couldn't see washing
their hair in deep green pools, I called

trees. If I had told you would you
    have known them?
                    There were
flowers for me. There
were trees. There were kinds
of birds and something blue

that crouched
                in the green day waiting
for evening.
If I had told you would
you have known?

So I sat
        on a bench among flowers
and trees facing
the traffic   surveying all

I knew of impalas, cougars, falcons
        barracudas, mustangs, wild
                            cats,
marlins, watching cars
go by.   I named them
    all.

Your Eyes Have Their Silence

Your eyes have their silence in giving words
back more beautifully than trees can rain
and give back in swaying the rain
that makes silence mutable and startles nesting birds.

And so it rains. And so I speak or not
as your eyes go from silence suddenly
at love to wonder (as those quiet birds suddenly
at rain) letting, finally, myself be taught

silence before your eyes conceding everything
spoken as experience, as love, as reason
enough not to speak of them and my reason
crawls into the silence of your eyes. Spring

always promises something, sometimes only more
beauty: and so it rains. And so I take
whatever promise there is in silence as you take
words as rain and give them back in silence before

there are ways to say that more beauty is nothing
for you before my hands can memorize
the beauty of your slender movements and nothing
is beautiful as words nesting in your eyes.

January 16, 1967: 5:30 PM

so that you will know where the sun was
   . Too cold to look up but going downhill
home, I saw the pink contrail, so high

it began the length of my thumb behind
   the silver nail, going somewhere northwest,
just going, like one of the kids running down the street

streaming long crepe paper behind just to keep
   it in the air. "Beautiful," I said,
committing myself, thinking about the

cold up there surrounding the pilot
   in the cockpit, comforted by warm
instruments and dialfaces. Then, more than

I could bear, another, coming from where
   the first was going, their flight patterns
giving them all the margin of safety

from fingertip to elbow, they passed—
   the ductile, malleable cold making
pink parallel bars that showed how pilots

go from where to when, and why horizons
   lose their distance between the points of going.
Forced into a judgment this time, I saw

that it was good and let them go wherever
   they were going, and let the sun go down,
and turned the corner home to my own warmfaces, and rested.

Obits

1. Deaths Yesterday
      I was alive yesterday but sleeping late.
    The sun rose in the same way
  and went straight down the path
behind the column of trees   outside my window

the leaves sucked the light in
breathed oxygen out   burned the morning away.

When I awoke this morning
the paper had printed in columns

the names of those who died after it went to bed
yesterday.

2. Previous Deaths
I have been alive since Friday but in my room
studying and writing and didn't see
the weekend. Saturday night the weather
turned cool.

Sunday evening I opened my curtains
and sat looking into the street   thru the trees

I saw the sun setting
on a girl walking far

down the street and I loved her.
This morning, Monday,

the paper printed the names
of those who had died over the weekend.

3. Deaths Elsewhere
I have been alive but dying
   in helms with crests like blue wheat
      wide-eyed shields   sliding blades   blood,mud
         sacrilege for the earth where no home is   monoculared

in wheeling vultures, the worship of jackal teeth:
choreography of sudden space, rope-rhythm under feet

bloodthick,penitent, eyesburst,tongue,penisthrust purged in kero-
   sene:
the suns, the million summers in immolation   suttees   doves

heretics of wood for stakes and chairs   bubble crinkle skin:
trials of water   suicide, flood   gifts of tongues

eyes, bones to the pearls and coral of the sea:
in mushrooms   mushrooms that blossom in my skies

my love   my   love   umbrellas c o ʌ e r our lives.

I awoke one morning late missing the world
got the paper and started reading thru:
all deadlines made   promises kept   I found it
in sect. 3, p. 4, col. 2.

Another Way of Dying

> The body's judgment is as good as the mind's, and
> the body shrinks from annihilation. We get in the
> habit of living before acquiring the habit of think-
> ing. In that race which daily hastens us toward
> death, the body maintains its irreparable lead.
>
> Camus, *The Myth of Sisyphus*

A whim is all it takes
and there's the race

a rape by the mind
makes shambles of temples
and images
         every day
nature fills her womb
with our dead
and blooms

with the elements of all our griefs like a mad girl with flowers.

The fingers and lips as tender as rain
below my belly feel my heart and
feed me the darkest warmest
moments of life.
Only the mind
would call
the turn
the other way and deny the truth I find when

my own hand turns against me where
the blood goes back and forth
below my belly
Oh
oh death where are you now?

You neither frighten nor
amuse the rain whose
soft voices still whisper
mutinies to spring
                    who breaks our hearts
more than you
                    with the indifference
of her green
                    forgiving eyes.

Letter to Cathy A

1

Again that perverse entity of relays
and my number .
that Saturday morning .
in bed with the life that let me go
and my sleep said hello and you sweetly
apologized into my conversational
trap.
The names to identify the idea.
Past them, we measured each other
wallowing in inches of flesh and hair
    stripped from our bones and displayed
    like relics from pilgrimages never made

    (Write me down   Cathy   write
    me down   )

True or not the numbers taped
switched relays
the entity breathed, audibly, with your lungs
"Jerry I want you to fuck me."

This time was it me?
Others claimed to have cunts
of every shape and hue thrown
a c r o s s their paths at every turn
that eluded me with singleminded malice.

Past arrangements, the telephone died in my hand
I waited and dreamed
holding the shape of your voice
                              palpable and warm in my mind
to let my fear-
                fully tender hands   like Pygmalion's
dream the contours of your words
and you were shaped to the shape of my hands
your breasts measuring those in my seraglio
of photographs   pornography   and calendars
your hair a crisp wedge to open your black thighs
and lips

and I was co-creator with your words and breathed
with you   in-
to you
shaped into the warmest crevices
    every syllable
                you were
bursting on every tongue of my body.

2

Black bees
the color of my new love's * *
                             * *

at least you say so
but I never seed it
yet
because I have my will
   in this terrible bed
your voice creeps out of my lickerish telephone
and grows in me
                day by night beyond the range of my waiting

Night by day what will
you do with the day
or I with the night un-
             adorned
             added to each other?
because your days
cannot be lived with out blindness or
my nights endured with
   out pity and terror
we can survive only in the beautiful twi-light of a lie
or the dawn of half hidden truth

only at the pt
          u i
         g
         h
          t horizon between us
can we **** with naked ****

and see O beauty-
full the day when my w*a*n*t*ing

be- C*O*M*E*S
                the night
                the color

as black as bees
                your * *
                     **
O daynight   (Give
O diynaght   (Sympathize
O dignayht   (Exercise
O dignathy   (CONTROL

dignathy dignathy dignathy

Because I will it
sister of my soul
I believe honey bees sweet swarming
black in the color of the * *
                          * * between your thighs
                           *

and your brown eyes
and your brown eyes
and your brown eyes
and your ravaging
        brown * * * *

    3
I have not forgot the foolish songs the rains sing
or the lisping choruses of the moon
and I know that dizzy leaves stagger down the air
scattering trills and grace-notes with wanton virtuosity—

I do not forget . and when you sing
I want the taste of your voice to fill my mouth
so that I remember how much the rain   and moon
and silly leaves hurt.

Now. and then.too. when I knew not
to take them lightly but kept even the hurt salted away
to season with spring and flavor with time
the years that would turn back to hear someone singing.

And didnt I turn that morning to the figure
your voice made and discover something dancing?
the way turning becomes a dance . the way spring
still dances . and I turn back and listen

and I know all the tunes and have forgot more words
than you have memorized. If you think of autumn
only as the foot winter drags behind
leaving furrowed scars across the feathery

green gardens of your summer mind
remember I can not atone for all the years I've lived
can not make the rain and moon and silly leaves hurt us
both   except by meeting you between the turnings

of our solstices . where we can remember all I have forgot
and give you . give you the words to remember
when you turn from your indian summer
to catch the sound of my distant singing.

    4
Not sleeping sleep now but doing dreams
socking it all night to the girl on the wall
I've had to substitute for a voice

and goddam you're the model
for this thing I've got about hair
(Ho for a rime! like who was it. . . . Baudelaire?)
and all night (or as long as I can take it)
I tangle & untangle weave & unweave curl & un
curl it around my   fingers   ?
among other things and I just
die

And you listen
and (dig) "steal into my soul"
and with our loaf and jug there
we lie—me reading my poems and curling & uncurling my fingers
"beneath the bough"   (did you)
                                                    DIG?)

    5
You did not come.
The time past   the room waiting   sheets still clean
again I waited
to be written down.

In these two years I've grown older   grow
less willing to believe in wrong numbers
I've made my own covenant with a rainbow
I've become one of those who woo

the seasons for promises never kept
share my secret lusts with the lascivious breezes that blow
me to my kingdom's come
and lap the dew under spring's green gown in lieu of you.

I've hoped to hear from you again
but life still keeps letting me go
In the mean time be-
ware of lonely men who need you

but if you read this and remember and want to meet me
still   please let me know
some how and I will come half way
be tween where I am and where ever you say

And if there are any heavens for dreams raised by
the voices of wrong numbers
I consign mine to whatever circle re-
served for romantic fools who
cant keep their cool and dignathy

(which means c o n t r O l

First Carolina Rain

and
so
this is the way
it rains in carolina
23 sept 69
school started for them
in pittsburgh too
and they dont need this kind of rain
especially my second son
the grave serious one
needs dry weather
to carry his busted arm to school
(glad I tried to teach all three
ambi
  dexterity)
need it or not
i carry the rain to school with me
sometimes seeing in student's black faces
my own sons
wondering how it will be to face them
when they reach this age

III ANOTHER KIND OF RAIN

Earthlog I

The Great Gift. we thought .
Even for Us the error was co
    los
    sal
to make them beautiful
so that beauty would please
    distract them
    as they grew
    and determined their destiny.

They did

To the majority we gave correspondences to seasons
autumn mostly
the range of their skins
skinsoft   the black earth   and boughs   browns   the trees   soft
skin   colors   the leaves

We were fair with the rest.
All those colors in their hair
    everything complementing them all

    not enough
    no ten ough
Things to play with. Baubles.
No more significance than a whim.
Lust of our eyes for variety . color . beauty .

They did.

(Maybe when love is in
                    fashion

The crew grows weary.
Oh, shit.
There are more alarms among the passengers.
Shiva wants to destroy them all
now.
J.C. says he will never go back
there.

America

My succubus smokes too much and hacks
all night at the intervals of our wall.

I've painted this side a color I call Black
to make a mirror for her
                    to see her withered cheeks

and I lie in/and wait for the end of her late show
and the last Transcontinental that rumbles

down and under the middle of our street.
How long can I wait for the end of her lateshow

listening for the voice that never answers her ?
(When I learned she has a cat
I stopped wondering who was more alone

   who will risk my room's dim circle
      butterflys brush the circle of my mind
      touching its chill
      loneness and fluttering down in bright ruins
      can my demon lust only at the risk of black love

   I hear her laugh at situations as her life bubbles
   out of her magic pot

until the end of the late show.
Her yawns warn when she will close the intervals

and put her dreams to keep warm in my sleep.
If I sleep
        she will expect my mouth to surprise her
        in her hair
        she will expect my tongue between her thighs
        will she accept degrees to prove how well
        the din of voices is silenced by touching
        it is done

Did the train bring her?
Did she ride the rails of the bright train
diving under the roads running under our lives?
Crossing my mind with shame in my blood,
in my mind crossing waves with amber   waving
fruit with plains,
prairies crossed from bridge to golden bridge,
crossing in my mind lovers with stars,
dreams crossed with promises—
once standing deepkneed in bayous I saw crossing
in my mind Columbus Balboa waving
from trains at my trackers,
crossing the horizon with smears of long black fingers—

She shows me the Golden Spike to prove she's made the trip
to drive us together
heart thru heart

        The show is over. Our beds are close
        but only her turnings came thru the wall.

I hear the old
slow train
moving
under us   around the detours she's made.
Silence opens her mouth when she sees I'm awake.
      I am not asleep   I am not sleeping
      and the gold between our hearts is black with our blood.

           (Trust me   demon   I am older
           than you   older than all your myths
           I had a dream

           that travelled farther than yours
           on bloated ships
           away from older dreams than yours
           to let you dream in me

C for Charlie

It's a way of keeping informed I guess
but I'm easier to get along with
if I can just get through the day with
out reading a newspaper. It's
the risk I take between Peanuts and Vietnam.
   Charlie Brown has to win a game soon
   for the sake of common decency or no
   body will believe in anything.

What I believe now
is that children would rather play
   in their own shit than with fire
the way Charlie Brown keeps burning them in there
and getting knocked on his ass just because he
   keeps trying.
   But given time enough he may prove
himself a quitter
and become a real kid
diddling himself and setting fire to cats
and other innocent small things.

   Do mothers
still hang gold stars in windows
for sons who burned them in there?
   This is known as success.
Patriotic grief is palpable and its taste is good
and Charlie Brown's ERA was out of sight
   anyway.

Third Dance Poem: In Slow Motion on a Split Screen

> The Greeks were cowardly in their fights, as most
> wise men are; but because they were learned and well
> taught, they bore their sickness with Patience and
> severity.
>
> Jeremy Taylor, *Holy Dying*

The football spirals straight up, rolling from the fingertips
    of the young onearmed
  intramural Greek who
drifts, drifts under it on the green wide campus.
    He is alone in the middle
  of his half of it, of course.
It has to be that way for him and the sake of this poem.

                    On the other
half the young Spartan chorus moves in one
    voice & speaks in cadence
  through tragic masks
for some of the citizens, older. "You had a good home but you left.
    You're right!" There are
  some angry young Athenians
who don't like it & want them off their half of the screen.
    The Academy is
  no place for this
sort of thing, they protest, & surround the field & pass
    out pamphlets. The one
  armed intramural Greek's
left sleeve is pinned to his shoulder. He doesn't
    care & neither do they,
  who won't look. He drifts
a little & snatches the ball to his side just as it touches
    his fingertips. Sometimes
  he throws or kicks it
away from him & runs his onearmed way to catch it.

When he misses, he shakes
his head, down, dis-
couraged. He cares about that. What good would one armed
Greek have been at
Thermopylae anyway? (It's the only
battle I know to mention except Hill 871,
or Olympus, as they called it
then, where the gods fought.
Let them. We try to bear our sicknesses without complaint
except in war.
The Spartans march across
the green grass again with shouldered arms. The Athenians
roar. The onearmed Greek
sits on the ground and tries
to tie his shoe. Our childhoods end in frustration.

Odysseus at the Mast

They lashed him halfway up the mast
And he screamed above the silent oarsmen
As they rowed him relentlessly away
From the bone-cluttered island shore of the Sirens
Sitting in the flowers singing unearthly promise.

> They saw the ship go by,
> and the madman raving there;
> one of them stood up,
> still singing, and made gestures
> with her naked body, using
> hands between thighs, showing
> as well as singing.
> The ship went on by wind and oars.
> The voice faded.
> They shrugged, sucked their sharp teeth,
> and went back to their flowers.

His anxious men, blessed with the silence
Of the blind, saw only the soundless agony
As he fought the bonds of the rigid mast
For the vision the Sirens never dreamed
In a world that faded for ever as he moved

Through life after life in the ship at the mast
And his screaming for release ceased.
They lowered him down among their flesh
And he mastered again his own flesh and his ship
And remembered, once, an impotent wish to mutiny.

For a Black Poet

BLAM! BLAM! BLAM! POW! BLAM! POW!
RATTTTTTTAT! BLACK IS BEAUTIFUL, WHI
TY! RAATTTTTTTAT! POW! THERE GO A HON
KIE! GIT'M, POEM! POW! BLAM! BANG!
BANG! RATATAT! BLAM! COME ON, POEM! GET
THAT WHI-TE BEAST! BLAM! BLAM! POW!
ZAP! BANG! RAAATTTTTTTATAT! BLAM! BLAM!

How many fell for you, Brother?
How many did you leave
in the alley ballsmashed
headkicked in by your heavy feet?

The things we make as men
are guns triggered more efficiently than poems
and knives / and targets for the fires.

Men make revolutions
Poems will bring us to resurrection

There is prophecy in fire
and a beauty you can not see
   a sound you cannot hear
   below the exploding level of your poems
                  dress to kill
                  shoot to kill
                  love to kill
                  if you will
                  but write to bring back the dead

And you are beautiful, Brother
not because you say so but because
black is the beauty of night a Black woman
the way a woman knows her beauty
   whose blackness falls
   softly from the spaces between stars
   who confirms our terror at her beauty in silence
and whose deepest blackness is the matrix
for the pendant worlds that hang
                      spinning from her ears.

And Black , like the swan
the shadow of itself who knows the secret
in the middle of its beauty is doubled silence
rarer than the white rush of lust
that led Leda's swan children
slouching thru their cycles of destruction.

The black panther.
His soft walk of lithe strong paces
a way of knowing   the hunter
                        the hunted

the beautiful) (silent (terrible beauty)quiet(terror
from   fear) the
panicked   (fear
beast / 's   (fear
crash / ing   (fear
bel / low   (fear and
ug / ly   fear

Beautiful as
a Black poempoetperson should be who
  knows what beauty lurks in the lives of men who
  know what Shadow falls between promise and praise.

The things that make us men.
Your child's questioning black fingers
touching you
is the poem
and more terror and beauty
because of the Shadow between you
than all your words.

  The way blackness absorbs   swallows everything
  and you Brother bring back up only upper cases
undigested at that

                              while beaten far below the level
                                of your voice
                              your life's deepest meanings lie
                                fallow.

What I mean is the way some things scream
at you   when synesthesia destroys   sometimes the beholder
                                            and the beauty
and the sense of beauty is not truth
and no longer hurts
and frightens instead of making us
feel its terror.

A Man and a Woman

And Lilith said
   act like a nigger
   leave me for another woman
   after I've put you thru school
   I'll blow out your brains
But did I
   I did
   she didnt
   she didnt
and didnt know about Whitman
   and Vaughan and Chaucer our patron
   saints who blessed us with things
   to talk about
and didnt know I took you to look for the fisherman's basket
   in the controlled environment of the observatory
   that weird flower
   I had remembered so long
   that I had seen the first time when you were running
   young wild thru your island
   seeing unreal animals scuttling into the jungle:
      the guard in the white cap
      directed us   Raphael   Raphael
      to that spotted flower
and didnt know that seeing
   great gold fish
   copper pennies
   in the pagoda pool
   we wished away 13 years of our lives
   Lilith Lilith
   in the pagoda pool
   copper pennies
   great gold fish

And there we were somehow
   after you were born somewhere
      when I was eight somewhere
      else and
   after one of us or both had done   this
      instead of that when we were supposed to
      or went or were sent here or there
      at the right time and
   after you had thought there was no such thing for you
      again
      and I had thought love would let me grow old
      in my own ways

we met: I met you.
      You were young in my ways
      in my mind, for my age.
      Now I am old again
      and I keep myself in shape
      to keep my stomach in
      but Shazam Shazam I know a lot of Trivia
      and you dont even know
                 who
         Mantan and Butterfly
                 were
And now
and now I fumble with flowers
and the names of things
because it's my job when you never ask
      to tell you what things are
   "   you lose words and reduce my pride in naming the world to
      the simplicity of "thingamajig"

and what we like is to show
        it is still beautiful even
        when we talk dirty about it
As a man and a woman
we tried   we made mistakes
God   we made mistakes
too   then you opened
and closed around my fumbling
and then zap zap the spark
between the fingertips and
the organs
and it worked
"   we talked about it

And it works

This Poem Will Say I Love You Before It Ends

Now, I am afraid to die.
This time and place. Our lives.
The end has changed the now,
this season of my life.
This time of my sun.

My reference, my continuum—is your moving.
Walk. Move. Go there and back. Anything.
I cant join beginning and end
unless you uncreate the tyranny
of all other absolutes.

We met in the thirty-fourth year of my life.
The end destroys the beginning.
I think about death.

Last night's climax frightened me with proof of my sanity.
Quieter than ever,
it locked us, and you stopped moving
and joined and confirmed Genesis and Apocalypse,
and I knew what time summer comes to the Pleiades
when it is dawn on Antares
when Orion kills.
I knew until the clock ticked again.
And you said oh and moved again.
I was there for ever.

In the thirty-fifth year of my life,
back from somewhere inside you, outside us,
I still love you. I have kept my promise.

The Quick

Every day the old Negro moves the sprinkler
about the lawn of the funeral home.
From my window I watch it operate.

The mechanical arm trips up and down
interrupting the jet of water, sending
tracers of transparent rounds revolving

over the green green grass, bursting
in crystal flak among the leaves of the small
trees that border the drive. Today

I had to dodge the spray along the sidewalk.
Where the lawn slopes down to the hedges along the
walk, someone had slipped on the grass, so thick,

so green, so wet, and their heels had gouged
long furrows in the rich brown
fertilized soil underneath.

At night

it's a quarter of a block whiter than anything
on earth. Surrounded by black trees
it blazes in its floodlights and sprouts
green green awnings at every

window and porch. Nothing goes out
or off all night except the twin
fountains in the corners of its wings that gush
sprays of synchronized red white

violet and yellow until two a.m.
Hung in burning oils inside, more
lifelike than real, the founder
looks out through his long glass-enclosed

entrance and trellised moss-hung
carport and accepts my tribute of surprise
each time I walk past at
night with benevolent vagueness.

There is a phone booth on the corner a little
past where I turn in. On a quiet
night I could hear if it ever
                                            rang

The Postal Clerk Mourns His Lost Love
(who has been going places)

"I love my baby, but my baby don't love me
I love my baby, but my baby don't love me
That's why this song is called
Things ain't what they used to be."

it always happens
I get sentimental
and remember old songs
(whatever happened to Cootie Williams anyway?)
and I wonder how in hell anybody
can get anything done
even if suffering is supposed to create
something
when I look for mail going to where
                                          she is

and send a letter for Ohio A-L God knows where

Fourth Dance Poem

In legend, the appearance of White Ladies usually
forbodes death. In Normandy they lurk on bridges
and other narrow places and ask the traveller to
dance. If he refuses the Lady he is thrown into a
ditch.

The White Lady has asked me to dance.
She had been lurking under the bridge I had to cross
   to go anywhere.
I've considered my answer
and since I've stopped denying it
                     she knows I have natural rhythm
so will she believe I dont know this dance?

"Why dance we not? Why stand we still?"

She has seen the white feather
I wear in my cap like a plume
and doubts my honesty
but I say to her anyway
ah White Lady
but I dont know this dance.

She hasnt believed me.

"They flee from me that sometime did me seek."

Oh White Lady
now you've said it

for me it was a long walk from Alabama

and I was on my way anywhere

[Untitled]

Not knowing what to do with themselves
because their thighs were equally soft
   because their breasts made no room for each other
not knowing they covered the sand

and the sea held in the voices around them
because they did at last

they discovered their hands held fingers in them
they surprised their mouths with tongues in them

found places for them
and cried be (

             cause
           (tween

) them they knew
men would say yes because they were beautiful (or not

and pain should not be wasted
and women no it is not enough

but because they did (not
they found room for each other on the bloodless sand

The Dozens

A Small Drama in One Act, One Scene

Big Boy   (Sophisticated, worldly-wise with the knowledge
learned from listening to the hip talk of other
big boys):
Yo momma yo momma yo momma
yo mom ahhh yo maaa yo mommmmmmmmmmUHma
momma yo yo mommamommamomm
ahhhhh yo momma yoooOOOOOHHHHH MAN
yo MOMMA!

Little Boy   (The Innocent who hasn't heard the hip talk
of the Big Boys. He doesn't understand why
there are tears in his eyes, but he knows,
vaguely, that he must reply):

An' . . . an' . . . and you is ANOTHER one!

[Untitled]

You want a lake
you want me
like a lake
to stand here
and give you back
single meanings
surrounded by the will
of the land to give you
your memory of still water

fuck you I'm a river
changing changing changing
watch how I'm changing
starting out slow
sluggish with scum
and all the shit you've dumped in me
from the shore
all the waste of your lives
I'm flowing
murmuring
roaring
flooding and freeing my memory from the ghettoes in your minds
away from the hollow winds
that balloon your gods over the surface of your memories
and comfort you with empty images for your memory of still waters

let the winds sting your gods blueeyes with salt
                              and dry their dripping hearts
for I have been walked by gods my surface tension couldn't hold
who sank down and walked the black mud rich
                              under my currents

and I'm changing   flowing around them below me
touching my edges
I run and surrender to high cold mountains and depraved valleys
lapping myself clean with the dumb worshipping tongues of animals
licking at the impotent joy of a child's wading feet
                                    my black mud rich
between the toes of gods and kids who sound me
welcoming me
back to my source

The Old Gory

1. (*red*)

Nice of you, white
of you to reserve some of the red
land for the savage
whose fondness for your hair was real-
ly a compliment second only
to his knowing in-
stinc-tive-ly
Eve's tempter's tongue.
   Amazing the things that creep
under your beds.
Now it's yellow reds.
The color of the land never changes
neither do the tongues
whether splitting truth
(with or with out treaties)
or chemical fire licking
tenderly   lovingly   the round snub-nosed faces
of the evil menace.
   Big of you to reserve the red
land for the children.
You giveth and you taketh away.
   Curious how you never noticed
the stripes of your bunting
matched and bled
the same colors as your white sheets
and the slave's back and ragged scrotum
and the wet soil under the bodies of black soldiers.
   It was red.
   The same as yours.
   It's the color of the land that never changes.
Funny now
that you should ask why.

2.   (*white*)

"The Bible is a book of race"
he said the white race he
said also that Jews are not
and the afterthought that Blacks
are not nearly human enough was un
necessary he smiled. The slave
traders, ships' captains, and plantation
owners smiled too knowing their good
books as well as he reading in comfort
that God was on their side every time
they laughed away some thing pretending to be
human

The dust of the earth was Robin Hood flour.

So now I've heard it after all
these years fall into place
and I can stop worrying how to tell
Christ from the Klansman
and why
you seem to dwell
so much
on your s*st*rs

3.   (*blue*)

you made me blue
with the color of your fidelity   not true
as my blues blue

                         . because you didnt listen
when black was blue was black was Blue/
s.
in what name do you color truth
                                    now
that Black is the space between people   ?

For Malcolm: After Mecca

My whole life has been a chronology of—*changes.*

You lie now in many coffins
in parlors where your name
is dropped more heavily even than Death
sent you crashing to the stage
on which you had exorcised our shame.

In little rooms they gather now
bringing their own memories of your pilgrimage
they come and go
speaking of revolution
without knowing as you learned
how static hate is
without recognizing the man you were
lay in our shame
and your growth into martyrdom.

Earthlog: Final Entry

Early in the voyage
we discovered idolatry among the passengers.
We tried to let them alone because we thought they needed it
but it's a small ship
and even with our guidance system its course thru Chaos
had been erratic
and they threatened destruction   in our names
even tho there was no jealousy among us.

We let them act out
their ceremonies and rituals to us
in the name of the names they called us
                              and they died in each other's arms
"beasts kneegrows honkies niggas pigs revolutionaries"
died on the altars of their minds
                    eyes fixed
                    lips snarling
                    hands locked
                    on crosses and crescents
We wept
and comforted each other
                    when they tore out the hearts of their sons
                    to please us
ashamed to be prophets and gods to fools

Now the sons of devils and slaves watch the stars
and navigate well
and call themselves "Men."

It is very strange to feel not needed
and our deaths or retirements
may be imminent

PITT POETRY SERIES

James Den Boer, *Learning the Way*
  (1967 U.S. Award of the International Poetry Forum)
Jon Anderson, *Looking for Jonathan*
Jon Anderson, *Death & Friends*
John Engels, *The Homer Mitchell Place*
Samuel Hazo, *Blood Rights*
David P. Young, *Sweating Out the Winter*
  (1968 U.S. Award of the International Poetry Forum)
Fazıl Hüsnü Dağlarca, *Selected Poems*
  (Turkish Award of the International Poetry Forum)
Jack Anderson, *The Invention of New Jersey*
Gary Gildner, *First Practice*
David Steingass, *Body Compass*
Shirley Kaufman, *The Floor Keeps Turning*
  (1968 U.S. Award of the International Poetry Forum)
Michael S. Harper, *Dear John, Dear Coltrane*
Ed Roberson, *When Thy King Is A Boy*
Gerald W. Barrax, *Another Kind of Rain*
Abbie Huston Evans, *Collected Poems*
  (Pennsylvania Citation of the International Poetry Forum)

COLOPHON

These poems were set in Linotype Times Roman, and printed from the type by Heritage Printers, Inc., on Warren's Olde Style wove paper. They were then bound into books in Columbia cloth. The book design is by Gary Gore.